The *Undercover* Business Woman

2nd EDITION

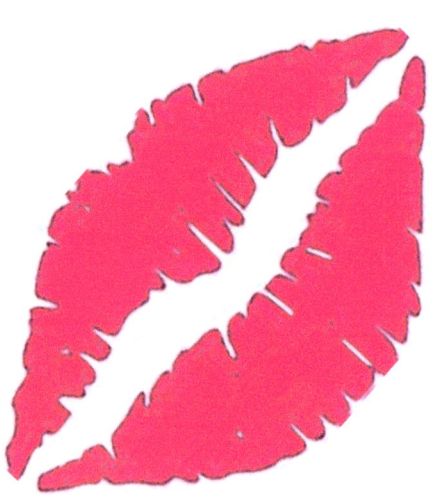

The *Undercover* Business Woman

Don't Let the Lipstick and Pearls Fool Ya!

Written by Angel Starks

'The First Lady of Comedy'

Cover Photo, Ashley Cox

Copyright

Copyright © 2016 by **Porshay K. Stegall**. All rights reserved. This book or any portion thereof may not be reproduced or used in any manner whatsoever without the express written permission of **The Butterfly Typeface** except for the use of brief quotations in a book review.

Printed in the United States of America

Second Printing, 2016

ISBN-13: 978-1942022-31-2
ISBN-10: 194202231X

The Butterfly Typeface Publishing
PO BOX 56193
Little Rock Arkansas 72215

To my 2 Mommies,

Ethel Stegall

&

Earnestine Snell

You two women are the reason I'm so fabulous — inside and out!

"Dwell on the beauty
of life.
Watch the stars,
and see yourself running
with them."

Marcus Aurelius

Fans

Fans, thank you! I can't be the success I was born to be without you. I'm destined to be successful so you're stuck with me - lol. When I'm on stage or at one of my book signings and look up and see your faces I see friends not fans. Please continue to share my world with me!

Dedication

To the absolute love of my life, Michael Starks, Director of Operations for Fab Life LLC. I don't know how I was ever living without you but I never want to look back. Thank you for all your support mentally, physically, financially and spiritually. I know it's hard to support someone who has a dream that's bigger than they are. Loving an artist and entertainer takes a special, handpicked man chosen by God - and you my dear have arrived custom made for me. I was afraid you wouldn't see me for who I am and couldn't picture the path I am on towards reaching euphoria, but it seems you do. No worries for me about what you want out of this life with me because you show me 24/7.

You were *crazy* enough to jump right in and now we are *crazy in love* for life 'til death do us apart. I love the thought of the creation of you. I am ecstatic about our love and I truly love you. The family we have together is epic. We are a team and I have a life partner in you.

You have witnessed me do comedy with a group of only 4 people staring at me like they had been tranquilized. That 4 turned into 40 and the 40 became 400 – all invested into seeing little old me, and *still* you were there.

Every good woman has to have a greater man to accommodate her and you do just that and more. I am so much more powerful with you by my side holding on to me and me on to you.

Life is still hard, but it's worth all the hard work knowing that when we reach high places you will be there by my side toasting with me.

People ask, "How do you manage a woman like her?" Your response is classic, "I don't manage her, I just love her."

What's Inside

Featured Growth

Shared Business Knowledge

Fun – Laughter

New Photos

Fan Photos

Author Information

Foreword

I have had the sincere pleasure of watching this young lady emerge into her own.

From early on, she was destined to be 'on stage', 'under lights' and amongst the stars.

Angel has such a 'gusto', 'go get em' attitude for and about life!

Mom, Comedienne, Model, Fitness guru, Amateur Photographer and now, Author – this 'Undercover Business Woman' can and DOES do it ALL. Best of all, she does it WELL!

Beautiful inside and out, her passion for life is demonstrated in EVERYTHING she does! I'm privileged not only to call her my niece, but also my friend! I love you Shay!
Fly beautiful butterfly, Fly!

Iris M Williams
Author/Publisher

Acknowledgment

Blessed Hand of Carmen Street - hair stylist, Shamara Cox - Business consultant, Regenold Dowdy – mentor, Marcus D. Wiley – comedy mentor, Personal Priority – wardrobe stylist, Ivory Duesron – hair & makeup stylist, Shanel Veonne – Clothes designer, Mike Ford – Personal fitness, Photographers: Stephen Brandon, Anthony Seymore & Mike Patton.

Earnestine Snell – Grandmother and architect of the foundation upon which I am built on. Curtis & Ethel Stegall – Parents (Thank you for creation). Takysha Simmons, Kalesha Swift – my sisters. Nieces: Jazz, Paris, and Bree. Nephew: Josh.

Fab Life Chicks for life: Destiny Brown, Carmen Street, Brandi Green Davis, Reese Miller, Shauna Gurly, Nikki Felder, Sylvia Baldwin and Brittan Ataberry. Thanks ladies and gents for coming out to all my adventurous events. Your faces give me the drive I need to succeed.

To all my people that I have shared a laugh or tear with, I love you all to the end and back again.

Iris M. Williams, thank you for giving me an opportunity to place my thoughts on paper for the world to read. Thank God I did the talking and you did the writing. I ain't gonna lie, I was a horrible grammar student. People would be like, "WTF is she saying?" Nobody's perfect. I do know sign language as a backup and if shit gets too uppity I will just finger my way through a conversation! (LOL)

Acknowledgment continued...

To my BFF's Destiny Brown, Brandi Green-Davis, Carmen Street and Shauna Gurly. You all have been some of my biggest supporters through it all. We all are equally busy women with families and careers, yet you ladies make me a priority and show up to just about everything I do. If you're not physically there, I know you're there with me in spirit. One of you is always by my side or in the background helping. That's love and I love you back for being who you are to me in this lifetime!

To my love Michael Starks - the glue that makes this puzzle called life stick together. Our children are amazing and hard work pays off.

My children who are my greatest creation. Nothing can top their existence!

My son Curtis Stegall, thank you for serving our country. I miss and love you. I'm so proud of you I could scream. You did it son. Know that even when it felt like I turned a cold shoulder, it was done out of love in order to help you see what I saw. I believe in you. You did it!

My three Power Puff Girls: Darlene, London and Paris. You girls are growing up so beautifully.

To my bonus children from God: Sabrina, Micha and Johnathan – I love you dearly.

Thank you to all my family that purchased a copy of the First Edition even though you already knew my story -lol! I would NOT have done that for you, but thanks - lol. *Just kidding.*

Faith McKinny Moore I have to personally thank you for your branding expertise and your vision. You have helped me get the attention and social media presence I needed, along with national exposure and opportunities. Thank you, we go way back and I'm proud of you.

To my publisher, Iris M. Williams, thank you for making me a Super Star ... one word at a time. I love you.

Shout Outs

Phyillis, Pigman
Jannifer, Denise
Julia, Marshall
Faith McKinny - Moore
(Branding expert)
Ashley Cox / Nine 23 Photography
(Book cover photo)
Brenda Jo / Reutebuch Photography
(Family holiday photos)
Nikki Blaine (Fashion Designer)
Sonny Bates (Movie Director)
Darvina Gallon – Friend & Supporter
Harold Hardy – Graphics Designer
Amps Magazine

Phenomenal Woman

Now you understand
Just why my head's not bowed.
I don't shout or jump about
Or have to talk real loud.
When you see me passing
It ought to make you proud.
I say,
It's in the click of my heels,
The bend of my hair,
the palm of my hand,
The need of my care,
'Cause I'm a woman
Phenomenally.
Phenomenal woman,
That's me.

Maya Angelou

Introduction

No matter how hard I try to deny an identity, I am STILL my mother's child. I see myself in her and I see her in me. I'm not sure how that can even be possible since we both are so dramatically different!

I fight daily to be my own me and not fall victim to my origins or originator. But buried deep down inside of me, inside that place I call my soul, the me that is my mother's child, yea that me - we speak.

Quietly we speak about the 'short comings', the 'over comings' and everything in between. She identifies with the me that wants to be FREE from a life that we created: kids, jobs, husband and family relationships thrown by the wayside.

I watch seemingly from far away, while she takes her new life on a joy ride. Yea I am my mother's child. I feel that, but I also feel the pain from watching from the side lines.

I am my mother's child and as scary as it may be – I embrace the wild streak, the beauty, the body, the gift to make people melt (men or women) like butter in my hands.

The *me* that I have decided to be has taken pain and turned it into power! I tamed a wild soul into a fierce soul - riding through life on cruise control taking it all in as I go.

When I reach my final destination there will be no regrets, no pain, no turning back. I'm taking my *power over pain* techniques and designing life that I plan to *marry til death do us part.*

I am my mother's child - stronger, smarter, and classier. I am the creator of all things in my life.

Diva

People keep calling me a *Runway Model Diva*, but to that I say, "No honey, I'm an Undercover Business Woman. Don't let the lipstick and pearls fool you!"

Angel Starks, The Undercover Business Woman

Look the Part!

> *"I don't care what people have to say about how I look. I know who I am and I'm not trying to win no beauty contest or a fashion show."*

I know you have heard this woman speak before. She is educated, gainfully employed, *usually* single and instead of makeup/jewelry, she adorns herself with a look of sadness and uncertainty.

Although she 'claims' that she doesn't care what people say or think, she really does. Not only is it evident by the sheer fact that she says she doesn't, but if you look into her eyes you will see that she longs to be respected and valued.

It may not be right, but it simply is a fact – people do care about people who care about 'themselves'. Are we looking for the approval of others – absolutely **NOT**. Do we want others to 'see us' – absolutely? I can prove it too:

The next time you see someone who you normally wouldn't compliment, take some extra time (it may take a while if they are looking an extra hot mess, but do it anyway!) to find something that's true and then compliment them on it and watch how their eyes light up.

No one is saying that you have to go overboard with makeup, clothes and accessories. What I am saying is that you must take care of yourself. You must take pride in your appearance. When you look good – you feel good! It's all connected.

If you're not into make-up, that's ok – but you should have a skin care regiment. If you're not into wearing jewelry, try a nice simple pair of studs, a single bangle and ring that can be a statement piece. And if your wardrobe hasn't seen change since the turn of the century – I am happily delivering bad news, "Honey its time to let the polyester and stripes go!" Invest in a few quality pieces that you can mix and match together and that will easily take you from day to night with minimum effort.

In the business world, the first thing people see and notice is our appearance. Heck, even when you're standing in front of a crowd delivering a million-dollar speech, they won't get past your introduction if the $5 thrift store outfit that you're wearing LOOKS like a $5 thrift store outfit. They will all wonder how they can trust you with their time and/or money when you clearly don't spend neither on yourself!

Keep reading and let's tackle this thing together. You need to know how important it is to look the part for the role you want in this life!

"Do Work!"

Angel Starks, The Undercover Business Woman

Be Authentic!

"I know I'm blessed! Do you? Everything I do, I know that I'm not doing it alone. I can't (and won't) take full credit for any of this. I have THE GREATEST business partner. He knows I'm not perfect – heck He made me this way on purpose! So my job is to be the best IMPERFECT person I can be!"

You can quote me on that!

– Angel Starks

Angel Starks, The Undercover Business Woman

The photo that started it all ...

Angel Starks, The Undercover Business Woman

Angel Starks, The Undercover Business Woman

L ipstick and Pearls mean something in my world. Accessories for the modern day business woman are like stocks on Wall Street – invest in quality in order to reap a higher reward later!

Ok so I've already established that I'm not perfect so now you won't be surprised when I talk about a few people. It's PG though (productive gossip) so it's allowed especially when you're trying to help folks. Here goes:

WHY are your shoes so tight? Your ankles *done swole* up and now you got rolls around your ankles that look like you're wearing rolled down flesh socks! Stop it!

Ladies, please don't wear a dress if ALL of you can't fit into it. If the dress has cups where your breast are *supposed* to go – then THAT'S the designated breast area, not above the wire or under the wire. And I've even seen this: the breasts both *above* and *under* the wire. Ummm, I'm not saying YOU can't fit the dress, but clearly your breasts can't and since *y'all* are a team – please move on to the next dress!

WHY is it that your hair sticks STRAIGHT OUT when you hold your head down? And WHY do you have enough 'beady beads' on your neck to shoot an army of folks?

I could go on and on but I think you get my message here. None of this stuff is cute and none of it is necessary. Stop buying/wearing shoes that are too small (Do you want feet like that RHOA star?)! Do SOMETHING to our head: go natural, buy some perm, a wig or invest in a weave! Throw broken jewelry away! And while you're at it – throw them STANK pantyhose out too! Gross!

Ladies, there is no excuse for trifling. If you don't have money for stuff – you just don't have money for stuff, but don't make it worse by substituting stuff with trash!

This is about taking PRIDE in yourself! Vanity and junk are at the opposite ends of the spectrum. God didn't make us to be poor. You don't represent Him when you look like you're homeless! God is about prosperity. He is king which makes you a princess! Act like one! No, better yet – be one!

Be Powerful!

People might change my attitude (I admit I am working on that part) but they can't touch my heart. I don't always smile and walk away when faced with foolishness – sometimes I may flick my hair, flash my lash or pop off a pink lipped comment just to seal the deal!

I keep it real but I rely heavily on my heart because it keeps me from forgetting who I am and stooping too low. "I love you heart for taking care of my soul. You allow people to see me even when this shell that is viewed as a brick house (lol) aka my body distracts the human eye. You, my heart, allow me to show others what seems to be for them, the 'unexpected' which is that I will do anything for others and that yes, my heart is bigger than my hair!"

Angel Starks, The Undercover Business Woman

On the flip side, you better come correct because I have been blessed with **SUPER PINK ANGEL POWERS** that allow me to see right through the BULLSHIT!!

You can quote me on that!

— Angel Starks

Weaves & Wigs!

Angel Starks, The Undercover Business Woman

Attitude

Everyone talks about how fake you are if you wear weaves or wigs but my take on that is this: how many of you wear deodorant or brush your teeth? Well, it's the same thing with wearing a weave or a wig – going without one (when clearly you need one) can mean the difference between people flocking towards you or running from you!

No one wants to chat with a foul mouth, musty woman any more than they want to see skimpy edges or those 'not quite making it' pony tails! Girl, if you pay for it – it's yours!

I have a BFF, Destiny Brown who swears by this. She says there may be days when she is feeling 'blah' and although she has nowhere to go and nothing to do, she gets up, puts on some lashes and throw in a quick weave and BAM just like that she feels energized! She puts on music and starts cleaning her house, organizing her closets and she says she feels like the most beautiful woman in the world!

It may be funny but it's not unheard of – if I have said it before, I will say it again – when you look good, you feel good! And when you feel good – others take notice!

When I worked in corporate America, I had so many friends you would have thought it was a social club instead of an insurance company. Women flocked to my desk EVERY MORNING just to talk to me. For the longest time I could never figure out why. One day one of my friends helped me figure it out. She said, "Angel, I love coming to your desk. You're so full of life and energy. Coming to you first thing in the morning is like having a strong cup of coffee – it just starts my day right!"

That's when I realized the benefit of a good attitude. Have you ever been in a bad mood or was feeling down and called someone to talk about it and they were down too? Before long, both of you were crying! I HATE when that happens. When I feel down, I make sure I call some happy people because sad people will grab you and hold you hostage with them down there in **Sadville** – *ain't* nobody got time for that!

My friend Carmen Street is who I call when I feel like I'm stuck in a mud pit. Carmen don't tolerate all that whining and stuff. She will say, "Girl gone on with that mess! Put on your big girl thongs (full briefs *aint* cute on nobody – big or little!) and walk it out!" Carmen says if you can do something about the situation, do it and if you can't – well fu*k the situation, the 'lame ass person' who brought it to you (y'all know haters always throwing salt and shade) AND anyone else who has a problem with it!

Well, alright then! Carmen always leaves me speechless. This *ain't* no different! Next!

Be Sexy!

"People wanna swing off shower curtain rods and nearly drown in the shower (I can't lie, it's happened to me before) but I say instead of trying to bring sexy back, how about we just keep sexy safe!"

You can quote me on that!

— *Angel Starks*

Sex Appeal

Ladies you can turn up with ya performance in the shower by hanging off shower heads and almost drown trying to have water run all down your face like the ladies in the movies if you want to (Lord knows I've tried it!), but as a grown ass woman I've learned a few things:

You can't buy *sexy* in the stores and you can't rehearse true sexiness. Sexiness lives within each woman. You're born with it and as you mature and grow, it will show naturally. It takes loving yourself inside and out, knowing who you are and having respect for everything about you! That's when true sex appeal will be revealed.

Yes, you can enhance your sexiness with clothes, attitude and sexy phrases, but it doesn't take all that to be viewed as sexy or to even feel sexy to yourself.

I've see plenty of grown ass women 3 times over the age of 21 shopping for some sexy at Forever 21 and they end up on my timeline with the fashion police looking for them. Now I *gotta* inbox my sisters and tell them they have a warrant out for public nudity and to lay low!

You know you couldn't fit them damn clothes when the tag said 'made in Korea' so why did you do it? I can't *y'all* and I won't.

Truly take a minute ladies and figure out how to let your natural sexy and beauty shine. It don't take all this extra stuff.

Unless you *tryna* hook a sugar daddy, go on and do you boo - *Imma* pray for you *tho*.

Angel Starks, The Undercover Business Woman

Fabulous

&

Photogenic

Angel Starks, The Undercover Business Woman

Confidence

I LOVE taking pictures! And you should too. Pictures are a great way to see where you are, where you're going and when you need to turn back and start over! Many mornings after I'm dressed, I'll snap a few 'selfies' just to gauge my swag and I am not ashamed to admit that there have been too many times where I take my 'thought I was too cute self' BACK to my closet for a 'do over'.

We are our own worst critics – that's true - but so what! If YOU think you're PHINE, who cares what anyone else thinks! That happens often. You see it all the time: a confident woman will strut her stuff wearing something that maybe YOU wouldn't wear and so you try to shoot holes in her confidence by saying stuff like, "Girl I wouldn't wear that!" Well guess what, no one asked you too! Everything isn't for everybody. If God can be ok with us *choosing* to follow Him, why can't you be ok with Eloise wearing that bit flower hat on her head? I mean if she wants to look like Miss Celie from The Color Purple then let that lady stay with *Mista*! If she is happy, then you should be ecstatic and encouraging, "Gone Eloise girl with *yo* Color Purple hat – I see you!"

A confident woman is a happy woman and a happy woman is a successful woman. This pamphlet is not about style because I recognize that we all have our own unique style. What I think is cute, you may think is horrific (You'd be wrong of course, but we'll talk about that some other time.) and that's ok. What I want you to do is get you SOME STYLE and be happy! Stop walking around looking like a sloppy man. Put on a bra. Wear some spandex. Add some color to your life and accessorize from time to time. Make yourself a priority and watch the magic that happens – others will make you a priority too!

"Fitness is a Lifestyle!"

Angel Starks, The Undercover Business Woman

"Life is Fabulous"

Angel Starks, The Undercover Business Woman

Photo Gallery

Angel Starks, The Undercover Business Woman

On these next few pages are a few of my favorite photos. Enjoy and gather inspiration for your own life!

Angel Starks, The Undercover Business Woman

I Am The *First Lady* of *Comedy!*

Angel Starks, The Undercover Business Woman

Author!

Angel Starks, The Undercover Business Woman

Actress!

Angel Starks, The Undercover Business Woman

Entrepreneur!

Angel Starks, The Undercover Business Woman

Professional!

Angel Starks, The Undercover Business Woman

Comedienne!

Angel Starks, The Undercover Business Woman

Relevant!

Angel Starks, The Undercover Business Woman

My mama once said, "Don't be like me, be better than me." I now understand and appreciate that challenge!

— *Angel Starks*

Family is Priceless

Angel Starks, The Undercover Business Woman

Family Holiday Photos

Brenda Jo
Reutebuch Photography

Angel Starks, The Undercover Business Woman

Blessed!

The Starks Family 2015

Angel Starks, The Undercover Business Woman

Love is Beautiful!

The Mr. & The Mrs. 2015

Angel Starks, The Undercover Business Woman

Dare to Believe!

Army Mom 2015

Angel Starks, The Undercover Business Woman

Dreams Come True!

First Lady of Comedy 2015

Angel Starks, The Undercover Business Woman

Be Strong!

"Anyone can do anything they set their minds to. Follow your vision. I suffer from dyslexia and I still managed to publish TWO books. Writing books, performing on stage and fitness is only a small part of who I am; the bigger, stronger part of me is my ability to allow someone else to help me in areas where I'm not as strong."

You can quote me on that!

— *Angel Starks*

Awareness!

Some men think because I'm beautiful they can say whatever they want to me. I used to allow it for the sake of professionalism, but one night during intermission at a Jamie Foxx Concert I reached my limit. "Your pulchritude is hard to miss," the guy said.

Well that did it. I threw my drink in his face, stomped on his foot with my red bottom stiletto and called him a PERVERT! As I waited on the elevator to take me to the garage, I used my smart phone to look up the word Pulchritude (Now I already admitted to *y'all* that I'm not good with words so …).

How was I supposed to know he was calling me beautiful or that he was John W. Thompson, CEO for Microsoft Corporation and part owner of the Golden State Warriors!

Lashes & Life!

Angel Starks, The Undercover Business Woman

Success

I want my life to be like my lashes: lengthy, luscious and non-irritating! Ladies I know you know what I'm talking about here. There is nothing worse than lashes that don't last past the night, make you cry or leave you feeling unnoticed!

The key to life is to be happy, healthy and be able to buy shoes every week! Yea, people will tell you that money isn't everything and that's true but let's be honest – it sure is something!

If you don't have money, it's likely you won't be happy because you won't be able to pay bills and you may not be healthy because if you get sick you can't pay for medicine or a doctor and without meds or a doctor – you'll probably just die a long horrible death!

Ok, that's a bit extreme but I think you get the point I'm trying to make. We all need money – that's just how life works. Most of us have jobs or work for ourselves and the reason we do that is to make money. Well guess what, having beauty AND brains is an UNBEATABLE combination!

Beauty will get you in the door 'faster' and brains will keep you there 'longer'. People want to be around people who care about themselves AND who are successful. Notice I didn't say RICH, WEALTHY - I said successful. Success is not defined by money. Success is attitude. How many times have you heard this: If you think you can, you will and if you think you won't, you won't. It's absolutely true.

Our minds are the key to it all. You must FIRST think you're beautiful. You must FIRST think you're smart. You must FIRST think that you're successful.

And then – armed with that information – go out and make it happen!

Be Purposeful!

"I'm walking in **MY** assignment! For the people who don't like it, don't believe I can finish it or have questions about it – you can forward all that to my Teacher, my Leader, my God. Go ahead – I dare you! I am doing an *Angel's* work, you go do yours!"

You can quote me on that!

– Angel Starks

About Business!

Angel Starks, The Undercover Business Woman

Opportunity

My motto is this: Never let business become personal. If I don't see an opportunity for me, I make my own. Being a business woman takes some acting skills. I have to look the part, act the part, walk the part and know the role that I play to perfection.

It's not about being fake it's about stepping outside of your comfort zone and being deathly afraid of the dreams you are going after. I'm terrified most of the time because I set high standards for myself. While I'm not positive I can reach them, I know for sure I will not reach them if I do nothing.

I recently realized just how *undercover* I am on how I handle my business. I was in the bathroom of my 9 to 5 sending invoices to clients for my shirts and books. I also solicited for a magazine spot, got a featured advertisement and digitally signed the contract! Who cares where I am handling business as long as it gets done - we are all satisfied.

I stopped working a 9 to 5 because I was concerned people wouldn't take me serious if I worked an office job. I thought I needed to be a full time entertainer. Thankfully I was set straight (to my face) by a nationally known comedian … "All the great entertainers had more than one job to support and help build their future." Hands down THE BEST advice I've gotten so far.

I took his advice because I was getting anxious over using my business account in such a *negative* way. I bought t-shirts, posters, pens and books all on a $45 bank account and in return received 3 insufficient fees in addition to paying back the money I spent. But it did feel great knowing that I was investing in me!

Later, on a book tour to surrounding cities, I made my money back almost 3 times over. My point is that sometimes you just *gotta* believe in yourself. Invest even when you literally have nothing to give! (LOL) Work for that return!

Even if I'm just hanging out with friends, I'm still *undercover* handling business by building a bond with the waiter in hopes of returning on her night to work and host an event. She makes tips and I get free space!

I had to learn to protect my brand. You can't do business with just anyone. Every opportunity is not for you. Learn the difference between who you are in business and who you are in your personal life. It could be a thin line, but don't cross it!

Make Up, Out & Over!

Angel Starks, The Undercover Business Woman

Your Persona

How many of you ladies wear make-up? Hmmm *hunh*, now, how many of you allow your make up to wear you? Your make up shouldn't change you into a completely different and unrecognizable person.

I mean really, if your baby screams *bloody* murder when you go to pick him/her up – that's a clue that you're doing too much!

I hope this pamphlet makes you laugh but I also hope it makes the point I'm trying to make. Know who you are. Know your value. Know your purpose and determine where you want to go and then – go get it!

Each of us were designed by God for a specific assignment. Mine is to make people laugh and feel good about themselves. I had several 'false starts' which is understandable because there are a ton of ways to make people feel good. I tried working in finance on an Army base, teaching at an elementary school, and was even a director at a child care facility. I *enjoyed* those professions but they didn't fulfill me like comedy does. There is something about being a comedienne. When you know something, you just know it! There is no limit to the life you can lead, except for the one you put on it.

Stop hiding behind excuses, nappy heads (unless you rocking the natural style – in which case, YOU GO GIRL!), chipped nail polish, worn shoes and tattered clothing. My granny used to always say, "There is no reason on Earth you should be walking around looking like you already dead and buried!"

If you have a high powered, high paying job take some time to reinvent yourself inside out and then from top to bottom. (True change comes from the inside first.) I guarantee you that when others notice that you care about you, they will begin to care too. Those promotions that you KNOW you're qualified for, but have eluded you for all of these years are just waiting for you to come along and claim them.

If you don't have the job you want yet or maybe you have one that is limited financially, and can't purchase high quality items - don't worry I have some good news for you too! Shop thrift stores (you can find some good buys there, hold out for them), consignment stores and even the dollar stores. Take care of what you have until you can have what you care to. Everyone has to start somewhere.

Start building your brand girl!

Truth

"My nose was running, I had bronchitis and my eyes looked like a raccoon had done my makeup, yet everyone kept saying, "You look great!" So does that mean I 'always' look like Roscoe from Martin?"

— *Angel Starks*

It's a Wrap

People will look you in your eyes, smile and then straight up tell you a bald head lie. That's why it's important to have that one girlfriend who will tell you when you are being foul even if you get mad at her for a while. (Ladies why do we get mad at the truth when we KNOW it's the truth!) Suck it up and then change your underwear!

The quote from the beginning of this pamphlet is a real one. I actually heard someone say that as she stood in front of a crowd giving a presentation. Now I don't know what the other participants were thinking but I know what I was thinking, "Why?" "Why are you looking like you looking?" "Why are you pretending that you don't know or care how you look? And "Why do you think WE don't see and are affected by how you look?"

I thought long and hard about her saying she didn't care and I wondered if she really didn't care! I suppose if she doesn't it could be that she's lied to herself for so long that she doesn't care. She's given up. She's checked out. She's one of the "Living Dead!" Yikes!

Ladies watch out for people like that. People who have already checked out are contagious because if you hang out with them long enough, you'll find yourself slowly checking out too.

I remember when I was younger (and more impressionable) I saw my neighbors leaving their home and going to the gas station or the grocery store wearing pajamas, house shoes and bonnets! At first I was like, "Why she doing that?" But the more I was around them, the more their 'rationale' began to make sense to me. I thought, "Well, it's only the grocery store and I'm only going to be gone for a minute!"

WRONG. I don't care if you're going to take trash to the dumpster – stop looking like you've escaped from the mental hospital on a Sunday night! If you do it once, you will begin to think its ok to do it often so better to just not go there!

So back to the woman who started all of this. You know, the woman who said she doesn't care what people say or think about her. Well, I reached out to her (yes I did!) because I want to help – if I can.

I asked her out for coffee and made sure I was looking my best. During the course of our conversation, I made sure to compliment her on something. (It wasn't hard; she was wearing pink which is my favorite color!) Then I told her that I am a licensed stylist (I am), a makeup artist (I am) and an amateur photographer (I am). I told her I was putting together a fashion show and needed some models for the show. At first she was reluctant but when I got finished selling ME (I'm just that good!), she was eager to be on board!

Angel Starks, The Undercover Business Woman

She showed up for the event and I transformed her into the woman she already was – she just needed a little coaxing to come out and play. Once she saw what she could be, she was eager to maintain it. We keep in touch and she is full of questions and I'm happy to answer. Hmmm, maybe that will be my next book, "How to maintain your fabulous new look!"

The moral of the story is this – be the best you can be and then go help someone else be GREAT too! Maya Angelou said so!

"When you learn, teach …"

Live Life

Angel Starks, The Undercover Business Woman

"Fit is Fine!"

Angel Starks, The Undercover Business Woman

To all the Phenomenal Women, put on your lipstick & pearls ... and then, go get your life!

Angel Starks, The Undercover Business Woman

Angel Starks, The Undercover Business Woman

Fun Fitness Facts

Angel Starks, The Undercover Business Woman

10 things you don't know about my fitness journey:

1. I adopted a healthy life style only three years ago.
2. I began my healthy lifestyle change after having chest pains. I thought I was dying - lol.
3. I'm Gluten free. I was diagnosed in a club in NYC by a drunk girl.
4. I chew gum 8 hours a day straight to burn 600 calories just doing my daily duties.
5. My heaviest weight was 155lbs at the time of my son's birth and 105 pounds post pregnancy. (Diagnosed with a severe gluten allergy)

Angel Starks, The Undercover Business Woman

6. I almost died in 2010 due to birth control malfunctions. Choose wisely because *your* life could depend on it. Do your research!
7. I eat 7 small meals a day to keep my metabolism up.
8. If I don't work out, I loose muscle tone which equals to me losing weight. I can't lose this booty so see you at the gym!
9. I started a Fitness company called Fab Life Fitness. I'm bringing fitness from the health club to the night clubs. I host Zumba dance parties in the clubs in my city.
10. I eat snacks, sugar, drink, overeat and miss working out some days. The trick is it's all in moderation. I don't get *sucked in* to my old bad habits. If I mess up I accept that and go hard the next day. Nobody's perfect so be the best imperfect person you can be.

Angel Starks, The Undercover Business Woman

About the Author

Angel Starks, The Undercover Business Woman

As far back as I can remember I've felt that I had the gift of loving people and making them love me simply by being me.

It helped that I was a tiny little thing, all dolled up by my stylist and my grandmother Earnestine. *Madear* as we fondly call her, kept me 'on point.'

I was a miniature 'little lady': well spoken, well behaved and polite were all the ingredients that made me a child celebrity within the small Arkansas town where I lived.

I remember feeling sick one day when I was about five. *Madear* dressed me in pearly white ruffle socks, shiny black shoes and a blue and white plaid dress that had a huge lacey collar. The outfit was completed by my head full of curls which had been rolled the night before with pieces of a brown paper bag. (We did what we had to back then which is why I KNOW there is

NO reason women should be lacking in the beauty department. Use what you have!)

As we walked through the town to the doctor's office people stopped us and asked me my name, my age and then proceeded to label me the most precious thing they had ever seen!

I was full of confidence at this early age but my grandmother kept me humbled by reminding me that if I acted ugly I'd be ugly no matter how cute I was. I was taught to have respect for others, treat folks the way I wanted to be treated but also not to let anyone make a fool out of me. *Madear* said if I didn't respect myself, no one else would either.

So I was polite, loving, helped others, made my opinions known and did my school work. I think that's acting cute because I continued to hold the title she is so cute and such a little lady *til* this day.

We never made it to the doctor that day because as luck would have it, the town grocery store allowed the photographer Olan Mills to set up his photo booth in the back of the store to take pictures of families and babies!

The photographer offered to take my pictures for free saying I was the most well behaved three-year-old he had ever seen in a grocery store and he loved my dress. (I was 5, but since the pictures were going to be free neither my grandmother nor I felt the need to correct him.)

That experience was my first memory of a professional photo shoot and I was in love! People came and stood around to watch me perform in front of the camera. I felt better and no longer felt the need to go to the doctor – lol!

I was healed by the love of people!

I have always loved talking to people and would sit on my grandmother's lap with a peppermint in my mouth, sucking my middle finger with my head tucked in her ample bosom listening to all the town's gossip. I suspect this is where I received my gift for gab.

I continued to take in all the life lessons that were given to me and as a young adult I began my life. When my first born –a son, came along I began to work in retail because of my love for fashion and people. I also opened my own small hair braiding shop as a second income so I could provide a more comfortable and quality filled life for me and my son.

As an entrepreneur, I felt powerful and I made a living doing what I wanted to do, how I wanted to do it. It was addictive and felt instinctual. However, soon my second child – a baby girl, came and I had to 'step up my game' and work harder. In addition to my braid shop, I began to take on other jobs.

Soon I was modeling, but when an opportunity came that required me to leave my babies for eight weeks I simply couldn't bear to be apart from them. This wasn't the first time I'd had to turn down a job because of travel so I made the decision to stop modeling and in 2009 began doing standup comedy.

Although I spent a lot of time with my grandmother, I inherited this crazy, wild and funny personality from my mom and my late father. I was dared to get on stage at Morty's Comedy Joint and the people loved me as much as I loved making them laugh. People who did not know me were 'giving me life'. I won the contest four weeks in a row! I say if you want to know if you're good at something, just ask a stranger. Family and friends my not tell you the truth because they love you and don't want to hurt you, but strangers – yea they'd love to throw a beer bottle at you from the audience!

I began doing private events and the money was good, but I didn't have a fan base. That would take time and commitment. Today, I am a full time traveling comedienne.

Labor Day 2015, I began my first comedy tour. I was invited to 'The Devil Show is Bizzy' tour by some great comics. If an opportunity is not offered to me, I find a way to make one for myself. I am self-encouraged, self-motivated and self-confident.

It took years of hard work, learning my worth and finding my gift and power over the human mind. It takes more than a heckler to break my spirit!

I am here to heal my brothers and sisters through laughter!

I am The First Lady of Comedy –

Angel Starks.

Fan Favorite Photos

The Empire Era

The Cookie

Look-a-like

Contest

Signing Autographs

Our versatile T-shirt

Our Products

Thank you
Fans & Supporters

What's NEW Since the First Edition?

This has truly been a whirlwind experience! From the time my feet hit the floor each morning to the time I crawl back into bed at night, this life is fabulous.

In the past few months I have …

- Filmed a TV Commercial
- Guest appearance on WishTV8 Style Show
- Appeared in TV shows Empire & Chicago Fire
- Appeared in several movies:
    - Chicago
        - W/ Rap Star Common
    - Age of Consent

- (Director Sonny Bates)
    - Love of a Lifetime
        - (Director Carmen Jameson)
- Guest appeared on two radio interviews with Radionext and Hot96.3
- Attended several Red Carpet Events, Two fundraisers and a Gala
- Met national opera Singer Angela Brown
    - Her jewelry line is called It's a Diva Thang (itsadivathang.com)
- VIP treatment on the purchase of my brand new 2015 as I was recognized as The Undercover Business Woman

Best of all I've gotten calls from all my family from Arkansas to NYC calling and asking to 'hold a few dollars'. I don't have no money y'all. Please pass it along and share this book with another family member so everyone gets the memo! (LOL)

I also went from having one Face book page with 300 friends to now three different pages and more than 2,000 friends! I'm trending now on social media y'all! (LOL)

I managed to even get the attention of Mark Zuckerberg! Well, the Facebook police locked me out of my page over my name and requested that I create a business page. I was upset at first, but then I realized that means someone is paying attention! (LOL)

I've lost friends and gained friends, but that comes with growing as a business woman, friend and public figure.

I look at it like this: I could meet someone tomorrow who has better intentions and understanding of who I am than someone who has been in my life my whole life ever could.

Time means nothing.
character is everything.

Comedy Shows

Were you there?

Did you enjoy the shows?

I want to hear from you!

Don't miss the next one!

Follow me in 2016

More shows

More comedy

More tours

Basically, I'm everywhere on Social Media, so come on and follow me:

Facebook Profiles:
Angel Starks
Undercover Business Woman
Fab Life Fitness
First Lady Comedian

Twitter: First Lady Fans
Instagram: comedienne_firstlady
Snapchat: comedianfirstlady
Email:
Contact Dewayne S. for comedy shows or book signings at:
theundercoverbusinesswoman@gmail.com

*Rest In Peace
Lorenzo Barnes Sr.
My favorite uncle…
Thanks for loving me, serving our country and setting a standard for success for the young men in our family.*

You Are STILL Here

Through the trials and tribulations,
you are still here.
For every door that was slammed in your face,
you managed to find a window.
When they told you, 'No it can't be done,'
you flipped the script and said,
"Let me show you what I can do!"
For every stone that was ever thrown at you –
you used them to build yourself up!
And now ... here you stand,
staring at a reflection of what THEY told you,
you would never be!

Latrea Wyche/Author
Green Tea & Other Forms of Meditation

The Butterfly Typeface Publishing

The Butterfly Typeface is a professional writing service company. Our goal is to 'spread a message' of inspiration, imagination and intrigue in all that we do. Whether you hire us to edit, ghostwrite, publish (books & magazines) or web design, you can be guaranteed exemplary customer service, fairness and quality. Our vision, under God's leadership, is to serve and assist in the healing of the heart, mind and soul of *all* people we encounter with integrity, intentional influence and positive purpose.

"We make good GREAT!"

Iris M Williams – Owner
The Butterfly Typeface
Little Rock Arkansas
www.butterflytypeface.com

www.ingramcontent.com/pod-product-compliance
Lightning Source LLC
Chambersburg PA
CBHW042321150426
43192CB00001B/6